New Principles of Awakened Relationship

New Principles of Awakened Relationship

Mutuality as a Dynamic Component of Our Awakening Nature

Rod Taylor

Awakening in Wholeness Publications

Sooke, British Columbia

New Principles of Awakened Relationship: Mutuality as a Component of Our Awakening Nature by Rod Taylor, edited by Ralf Humphries, PhD.

© Copyright Rod Taylor 2015. Second edition 2018.

10 9 8 7 6 5 4 3 2 1

Published by:
Awakening in Wholeness Publications
Sooke, BC
CANADA

email: awakened.relationship@gmail.com
www.awakened-relationship.com

Cover photo and format by Andrea Bruecks, MD and Rod Taylor
Cover titles, text layout, transcription and book concept by Ralf Humphries
Editing & book design by Ralf Humphries and Rod Taylor
Proof-reading & editing suggestions by Andrea Bruecks
Afterword photo by Rod Taylor
About the Editor photo by Shuwana Shiraze
Back Cover insert by Andrea Bruecks

Printed in the United States of America

ISBN: 978-0-9940356-6-0

To my beautiful wife Andrea Bruecks

who is reflected throughout the pages of this book

and is alive within the nature of my heart

Contents

PART II. LIVING AWAKENED RELATIONSHIP

PART III. EVOLVING IN FULFILLMENT

Introduction

RALF HUMPHRIES

ROD TAYLOR IS a human development teacher with a background in a broad range of approaches to spiritual growth pursued throughout the length of his adult life. His path eventually found its fulfillment in the form of a fundamental awakening shift into non-dual conscious embodiment in 2005, catalysed through his engagement with Saniel Bonder and the Waking Down in Mutuality® work. Rod became a teacher in that work in 2007, and he is now a teacher of Trillium Awakening™ .

In the course of his awakened life, Rod Taylor has come to articulate a teaching that reflects roots in the Waking Down and Trillium work, and at the same time expresses unique perspectives, discriminations and personal discoveries arising from his awakened nature.

IN *NEW PRINCIPLES of Awakened Relationship*, Rod Taylor shares with us how a newly emerging paradigm in the field of human development is bringing to light the significance of an interpersonal dimension that we can call 'mutuality'.

In this time, perhaps for the first time, human beings are coming together in the spirit of mutuality, meeting others, meeting themselves, and awakening in a way that is radically inclusive of *all of who we are* — in our finite embodied natures, in our spacious conscious natures, and in the nature of our interconnectedness to one another and to everything.

This 'whole-being' awakening has emerged at this time, catalysed by the recognition of mutuality as its igniting spark. No longer does spiritual growth primarily need to be activated and pursued in solitary, somatophobic practices, but the next step of our life's evolutionary unfolding is enlivened instead by getting together with others in groups, or with teacher-activators, seeing others and being seen by others as *okay* — just as we are.

Whole-being realization, seeded in the womb of mutuality, then opens up the territory of awakened *whole-being relationship*. And this is where Rod's awakened expression is a realizer's revelation of new principles that are at play here.

In this book, Rod gives particular attention to close, loving relationships, where the alchemical potency of the field of love amplifies the opportunity for discerning these new principles. Attending to the subtle and elusive interplays of interpersonal relating, and referencing his own lived experience, Rod brings to light in careful detail an evolutionary process in relationship emerging from the very nature of awareness itself.

In this new territory of whole-being relationships, the maps and familiar frameworks used by many contemporary relationship experts to address the challenges of up-close relating become less helpful. Traditionally, teachers on the topic of relationship emphasise, for example, restorative communication processes, or cooperative strategies between partners, or perhaps they want us to focus on the implications for couples of recent data emerging from research in neuroscience. While these are valuable areas of learning from which we have all benefited, Rod's book is revealing how the interpersonal field of mutuality, without a requirement to implement strategies or practices to fix or change ourselves, is bringing about a natural discovery and deepening in the living of relationship-as-love.

The transition in human development that Rod vividly elucidates for us here opens towards recognition of a relationship process more and more surrendered to the mysterious emergence in Being of a natural and trustable *dynamic-of-love* between people.

In intimate relationships and loving friendships alike, this dynamic of love brings, for each person and for the partnership (or friendship) itself, a unique evolution through ever-deepening awareness and integration into the full flowering of whole-being, heart-awakened life.

As a collaborator in the creation of this book, and as someone who is living in my own way the evolutionary life-processes Rod illuminates here, I want this offering to be a wonderful support for you as you make your own, hitherto unknown, discoveries in the field of awakening and awakened relationship.

Wishing you well,
Ralf

Ralf Humphries
Melbourne, Australia

Preface

WELCOME TO THIS OFFERING of realizations and perspectives on awakening and awakened relationship

As we grow toward non-dual conscious embodied awakening, we can become aware of an emerging ground of wholeness and love that offers, and indeed requires, awakened principles of relating. Mutuality (interconnectedness) comes to be revealed as a component of our own embodied, heart-awakened nature, with increasing capacity for meeting others in openness and love. With this realization, sharing with another in the discovery of wounds, confusions, and fulfillments in an awakening relationship can provide an alchemical cauldron for interpersonal growth and enrichment.

Whole-being realization is naturally occurring in humanity through many personal backgrounds, traditions, teachings, and practices. While my own path of personal and spiritual development found its fulfillment through a particular form of whole-being realization work, my hope is that what is offered here may be of value to anyone who finds themselves growing in embodied wholeness and navigating the field of relationship. Mutuality seems to me to be a new frontier in awakening realization.

This presentation is particularly relevant for those who have already come into their own conscious embodied awakening, or those who are experiencing this realization emerging and have come to recognize and trust the evolutionary processes of Being operating in their unfoldment. While traditional and modern approaches to interpersonal communication, shadow work, and relationship skills are not to be discounted, the shift into embodied awakened life provides a capacity for living 'new principles' that support the evolutionary unfolding of relationship in wholeness, trust, and love.

May you find resonance with expressions in this material that enliven your own awakening and integration, and that enhance your experience of awakening and awakened relationship!

With love,
Rod

Rod Taylor
Victoria (Sooke), BC, Canada

Acknowledgments

I AM SO VERY GRATEFUL to my beloved wife, *Andrea Bruecks,* for 'seeing me' and inviting me to join her in creating together a shared 'third entity' — a deep, bonded, love relationship. Andrea's grounded, unshakeable love has provided the current and catalyst for our evolving love partnership and a basis for my discernment of new principles of awakened relationship. It has been wonderful to share in this dance of discovery with Andrea as we deepen in love-trust together.

I want to express my deep gratitude to *Ralf Humphries* for his desire to make my ideas available to others: his creative initiative to record, transcribe, and edit my presentations; his creative intelligence as a producer, director and editor in the project; and his technical and graphic expertise for producing this beautiful publication. Our collaboration as he led us through the details of this project and supported my adjustments, refinements and additions, was richly rewarding. I so much admire Ralf's sensitive heart, wise intellect, and deep grasp of these ideas. I greatly enjoy our ongoing heartfelt, adventurous conversations and I treasure our loving connection.

Saniel Bonder and *Linda Groves-Bonder* have been an inspiration to me for living an awakened relationship. Saniel's realization of mutuality as a component of conscious embodied awakening, and his modelling of a masculine role in awakened love relationship, have provided the ground and illumination for my awakening, my teaching role, and my unfoldment in awakened relationship. My deep love and gratitude flow to Saniel and Linda for their teachings and their friendship.

My spiritual path and my role as a human development teacher have been significantly influenced by *Maharishi Mahesh Yogi*, founder of the Transcendental Meditation® program, and *Ou Wen Wei*, founder of Pangu Shengong qigong, both of whom I hold in deep appreciation and love.

My ideas in this book evolved and clarified while preparing and delivering workshops for numerous communities from 2010 through 2017. Those teaching opportunities came through invitations from welcoming *organizers, co-planners, accommodation providers,* and *participants* in: San Diego, Atlanta, Somerset (NJ), New York, Boston, and Olympia (WA) in the United States; Canberra, Sydney and Melbourne in Australia; Salt Spring Island in Canada; and Pattaya in Thailand. My heartfelt thanks to everyone involved!

I also want to express my deep love and appreciation to my children *Brahm, Luke, Archer,* and *Teylea,* who have profoundly enriched my life with fullness, learning and purpose, while following their own distinctive paths of awakening and love. I want to offer my admiration and love to my siblings *Pamela, Bill,* and *Gregg,* who are beautifully living mutuality in their own lives, and who have gifted me with their unwavering love, respect and care. And I want to express my gratitude and love for my parents *Harold* and *Ruth,* who provided me with

life, security and loving care, while modelling living with good-
ness and faith.

NEW PRINCIPLES OF
AWAKENED RELATIONSHIP

PART I

Awakening In
Mutuality

1

Awakened Mutuality

". . . we find the center of knowing and love is . . .
in our whole being. . . ."

THROUGH MY EXPERIENCES with people engaged in whole-being realization work, and also in my personal life — particularly in love relationship — I've been discovering more of the nature of awakened interpersonal connecting. And I'm finding that there are different principles at play. These principles of 'awakened mutuality' don't need to be discussed in relation to intimate relationship in particular, but nonetheless that for me is the most potent place where I meet the other as my normal self, in real life and in real time. It's the place where I am most likely to meet the other, not with an intentional behavior, but spontaneously moment to moment. So it's been a wonderful field for me to discover what, in my view, are *new principles of awakened relationship*.

When we consider the field of relationship, I've found that, in whole-being realization, *mutuality* is a dynamic component of our awakened nature. Awakening is no longer a matter of going to the cave or ashram to be primarily in consciousness. Whole-being realization actually requires living in life in connection with others and discovering the capacity to bring enlivenment of our consciousness right into our bodily, emotional, relational nature. And so we find that the center of knowing and love is in our *whole* being. It's not located just in the head, the heart, or the belly, for example, but it's all encompassing in our nature.

As a result, I am not just 'in myself', and I am not just 'in relationship.' I am actually both knowing the ground of life arising as me and as everyone, and I am recognizing the individual difference of every point of creation — which includes every other individual, as well as animals and trees and stones.

Hence, we can richly recognize that transcendent value of life and *simultaneously* find that it's manifested into form — form that itself is not *not* the absolute, but actually *is* the absolute in its manifest form. And when we tune into the conscious nature imbibed throughout our whole being, we find that that continuum of manifest and unmanifest is true of everything.

Acknowledging our relatedness with others, and indeed with everything, can be a path to discovering more of the wholeness of our nature, which is within us, 'outside' us, and among us.

2

Meeting in Mutuality

*"This relational dimension
brings a profound fullness
to awakening . . . ."*

IN THE CONSCIOUS EMBODIED awakening work that I teach in the Trillium Awakening™ path, *mutuality* is an essential form of support for the unfoldment of whole-being realization. In this work, there are intentional ways of 'doing' mutuality. These include regularly meeting one-on-one in sessions with teachers and mentors of this path, eye-to-eye mutual gazing in pairs during personal sessions and group events, and coming together in groups to meet with others engaged in this work in a particular way that we call 'mutuality.' We meet other people as they are, and honor the discomforts, the challenges and the goals of each person, and, crucially, allow people to feel *what it's like to be them being seen by others as not needing to change*. We meet each other in human equality, open-hearted, willing to hear and learn from the other, and open to having our understandings and positions change in the interaction.

In this way we nurture participants toward their self-realization through hearing, supporting, respecting, accepting and loving them. In particular roles, we also gently offer facilitating, mentoring, teaching and coaching support. As they awaken and find themselves evolving more autonomously in their awakened life, there may also be value in offering more proactive or directional guidance. However, in keeping with mutuality, we must still heartfully honor the human equality, mysterious life path, and different self-knowing of the other.

Saniel Bonder, author of *Healing the Spirit/Matter Split* and co-founder of Human Sun Institute, has been a pioneer in recognizing that whole-being non-dual awakening is inclusive of this dimension of mutuality. The Trillium Awakening path is informed by the Waking Down in Mutuality® principles that he developed. His realizations and insights have given rise to an approach to awakening that deeply embraces mutuality. This relational dimension brings a profound fullness to awakening, specifically *conscious embodied* awakening — so much so that we can speak about this interconnected awakened realization in terms of mutuality and love.

With this approach we have found, sometimes for the first time, that we can come together with others and talk about what it's really like to be us — with our hurts, our confusions, our pain and our anger — and actually have others hear us, without them saying, "Well, actually, you should do this," or, "That choice wasn't so good." Instead, they say, "Wow, that sounds awkward", or "Tell me more about that." In this way, we begin to investigate, and we find that those elements of ourselves that we thought were wrong, and which we were trying to fix or change or get away from, are actually innocent dimensions of us. And, when we deepen through these dimensions, we find more of a ground of aliveness that is arising as us. So we start to awaken in and through these innocent dimensions of ourselves and to realize this infinite field of Being arising as All That Is.

Coming into this field of mutuality, and finding these ways to meet with others that actually support this awakening, we are in a sense *practicing* mutuality. And deepening in this inter-personal mutuality dimension has been a significant component of the awakening process for all of us who have found our way into this kind of work, and found ourselves coming into greater wholeness through consciously meeting our own dis-comforts in the presence of others.

3

Doing Mutuality and Being Mutuality

*"... mutuality becomes an awakened component
of what we're discovering is ... our whole nature."*

THE SENSE OF 'DOING mutuality' is both an attitude and a way of being with each other that works beautifully when we are choosing to do that in groups in the way I've described. And so it's tricky sometimes when we go back into our personal lives. We want to be 'in mutuality' with our friends and with our family, and yet we are also just who we are. And, being who we are, we have reactions. It gets confusing because if we force ourselves to be in mutuality — hearing the other and so on — we are often not hearing what's happening inside us. Instead, we are almost artificially *holding ourselves separate* from our own discomforts, and from those of the other.

What I've found in this awakening process is that the 'practice' of mutuality emerges into our awakened nature in such a way that it is no longer a practice of 'doing' — mutuality becomes an *awakened component* of what we're discovering is in fact our whole nature. So we begin to have 'awakened *in* mutuality.' This is to say that we have awakened to the clarity of our own interconnected nature as both infinite and finite — and intrinsically complete.

When I use the word 'complete' here, it's to convey a recognition. I am liberated from the belief that there's something fundamentally incomplete about me — that is, something fundamentally wrong with who I am — because I've recognized that I am this dynamic of life-arising, which includes the unchanging field of all-that-is, and which has at the same time very specific limits of myself — for example: I may like chocolate ice-cream, but not vanilla; some personalities I may be more attracted to and not to others; I'm more of a scientist, or more of an artist.

So I can fully live into my individuality, because I'm not limited by *only* being that, I'm also all that's arising as me — and all that's arising as everyone. Moreover, I want to be that wholeness in the presence of others. And there isn't a conflict as I (and as each of us) discover this autonomous awakened nature. It's 'autonomous' because I don't need to find my nature outside of myself, but rather I'm actually just living it. I'm not prizing my individuality and my finite nature as being perfect, I'm just prizing it as my particular expression of Being.

4

Individuating Self

*". . . there's an evolutionary impulse in humankind
towards realizing an individuality
that is not separate. . . ."*

THERE IS A BEAUTIFUL way for us to recognize this current unfoldment in mutuality as an evolutionary outcome of the process of individualization that has characterized human evolution leading up to this time. However, an uncomfortable result of this process for humanity has been an increasing sense of split between spirit and matter as we've come (more or less) into this individualized stage of life. As we've realized more of our individuality, and more of the awareness components of 'observation' and 'witness,' we have become chronically separate, dissociated — 'split' in a sense. So we find this quality of splitness throughout the world: our sense of good and bad, for example, or hurtful conflicts that arise between people who each think that they are right, or technological progress that is helpful to humanity while damaging the environment.

Now, at this time, there's an evolutionary impulse in humankind towards realizing an individuality that is not separate from others. And it's not an intellectual process. Nor is it specifically through going out and finding others to connect with that this non-separate individuality is realized. It's actually through connecting with ourselves, through meeting the discomforts within ourselves — the challenges, the mysteries, the confusions — and finding ourselves in the process awakening to a field of realization that both honors our own awakened nature, and also, we discover, is non-separate from everything or anything.

Interestingly, being non-separate doesn't diminish the individuality of each point of creation, and each other person. The practice of mutuality is a beautiful one precisely because we're giving ourselves a chance to practice *that which in reality we are awakening to*. We are awakening to the fundamental recognition that it's okay to be me and it's okay to be you. And as we meet like this, supportive of each other, we deepen in such a way that we begin to discover this 'beingness' or aliveness arising as our self, and start to see in the other that deepening and beingness which they are discovering also.

5

Relationship Expectations

". . . we discover a new dimension of relating, . . .
meeting on a 'feeling' level
of mutual recognition and respect."

WHAT I'VE REFERRED TO as a 'process of individualization' has perhaps been humankind's most recent paradigm of development. So, from a paradigm characterized by the individuating self with a lived sense of split between spirit and matter, we find ourselves shifting into this whole-being paradigm of awareness and embodied awakeness-in-life, which has different principles at play.

From the spirit/matter split perspective, when we look at the individual and at relationship, we find ourselves in a state of separation that is reflected in our identification with our individuality, with our ego, with our mind, with our future desires, and with our need to be more. We are identified with them, and indeed they *are* a part of our progress and our evolution in life.

Then, when it comes to our natural attraction to be in relationship with others, there are the expectations of what that should be like, and it is painful if those expectations are not met. So we try to cooperate with each other in order to meet them. But in all of this there is a sense of *codependence*. And I don't mean 'codependence' necessarily in the pathological way that it's often talked about, but a certain kind of codependence: that, unconsciously, *we need our inadequacies, our hurts, to be met in the relationship, and somehow saved by the relationship.*

Hence we *need* the other, and we're connected by our limits in some cases — unconsciously. We don't notice it quite like that, so we say something like, "Oh, that's such a beautiful person!" Or, "This is perfect!" But what we find, often enough, in the depths of a longer period of time with someone, is that there are these recurring places that feel like weaknesses on our part, and there we expect something of the other. And, in the same way, they expect something of us. It's a tug of war that can sometimes be supportive in meeting life-challenges (when we are able to), but in truth we're still codependent, because we are not whole and well in our nature. There is a split in our nature, and the split is mirrored in the relationship. And in both dimensions of our life it's natural for us to not want to be split.

So if we find our way into a mutuality-based approach to whole-being realization, we can discover a new dimension of relating which doesn't try to fix the other, or have them fix us, but is more a meeting on a 'feeling' level of mutual recognition and respect. In this way, we begin to give a new meaning to love. Rather than feeling what we call 'love', and then experiencing the way that feeling is counteracted at times when we're not completely fulfilled by the other, instead we start off by noticing the *difference* of the other, and then experience love in respecting the other *as they are*.

6

Transmission, Resonance and Love

*". . . our being begins to vibrate more in harmony
with our wholeness than with our separateness."*

THE FIELD OF MUTUALITY includes a dimension some-times referred to as 'transmission,' or perhaps 'resonance.' These terms refer to an awakening *influence* or *activation* that may arise from our relationship with those who have become well-integrated in their own conscious embodied awakened nature (typically awakened teachers and mentors, and others well-seasoned in their whole-being awakened life).

These individuals have come into this awakened stage of their life typically through a process of deeply meeting their own inner condition over and over again, with the help, support, and resonant influence of trusted teachers, mentors, and peer group members. Their inner work has led them to a simultaneous real-ization of awakened consciousness, conscious embodiment, and non-separate interconnected wholeness — mutuality. They've come to realize their infinite nature as thoroughly intermingled with their finite nature, such that they express (or radiate) a quality of wholeness that is not the product of an intentional behavior, but is a condition of Being.

We can talk about those who've had this awakening as having had a 'whole-being realization' ('second birth') and living an awakened life ('second life'). These terms reflect the emergence of a paradigm characterized by whole-being realization from the previous paradigm of individuating self, an event uniquely expressed in each individual awakening. In living this new par-adigm, there is a simultaneous recognition of the infinite (or Being) and a respectful recognition of manifest individuality. As this conscious embodied realization deeply integrates within them during the initial months and years of their awakened life, they become a radiant source of whole-being activation for those who are drawn to it.

Thus, in whole-being realization work, we can be activated in our awakening both through an experience of mutuality in our interactions with *trusted* others, and through a resonant transmission in relationship to *awakened* others. In this resonant transmission, our own being can *feel* the wholeness in the other — and our being begins to vibrate more in harmony with our wholeness than with our separateness.

This resonant transmission can also be considered mutuality, because it is not really being 'done' by one person to the other; it is more an experience of resonance with the other. And in my language, that's actually a dimension of *love*.

7

Simultaneously Limited and Unlimited

". . . there is a relaxation into the joy of
not just the infinite dimension,
but also the joy of being
the individual, limited person."

THIS EMERGENCE INTO our whole-being awakened nature feels fresh at this point in human history. In it, we discover the dynamic process of a conscious, unchanging dimension that itself arises as life in all its expressions. We find that life itself *is* That, and we see that the 'limited' and the 'unlimited' are intermingled in such a way that there is no longer a need to retreat into consciousness to escape the confusion of our limits. Indeed, we actually find the 'unlimited' being simultaneously the 'limited'. In the midst of that paradox we discover a greater richness in our own being, and a greater richness — a *manifest* richness — in our interaction with every other person and every point of creation.

So, from identification with our individuality, and our more split condition with respect to the universe, there is a movement into a wholeness that is inclusive of both the infinite *and* of our finite limited nature — which is changing, which has hurts, which is in the process of development, and which will progress towards aging and dying. When we are in the separated condition, there is such a sense of things being wrong, and we want so much to hang onto life, and it seems so crucial that we find our way to perfection. But, in moving into the field where we recognize that this life process is actually Infinity or Being arising as us, there is a relaxation into the joy of not just the infinite dimension, but also the joy of being the individual, limited person.

8

Manifest Love

". . . we are knowing the oneness of Being
and the difference at the same time.
And we meet that difference with awe. . . ."

ACCOMPANYING THE DISCOVERY of our simultaneously infinite and individual nature, there is the joy of being this finite, individual nature meeting the infinite and the finite in others. Ahhh! It's exciting because we are meeting the known *and* the unknown. This is the field in which we get to play and experience *manifest* love. Rather than just realizing our infinite nature — the transcendent truth that we are this infinite consciousness in which all material differences are illusions — instead, we move into a condition in which both are valid, and we can hold both: the 'both/and', the infinite and the finite.

As a result, we get to know the field of love, or perhaps the 'fabric' of love, which seems to be the nature of fundamental existence from what I can tell. And we get to experience this whole range of being individual, because nobody knows exactly what it's like to be me, and nobody knows exactly what it's like to be you.

So, in a sense, we are knowing the oneness of Being and the difference at the same time. And we meet that difference with awe, for it's the space of the manifestation of love. Its the field in which the 'manifest me' and the 'manifest you' are meeting, and meeting in mystery. And when it is truly mystery, the other can't behave in ways we want them to. They are going to behave in ways that they *are*. And so are we! Here we begin to find the magic of seeing Being arising in a mysteriously different form.

9

Autonomy and Wholeness

"We have actually discovered for ourselves
that our nature is . . . universal Being."

THE MORE WHOLE we are, the more *autonomous* we are in our awakened nature. We're 'autonomous' because we don't need to get the essential data about our own nature from others, and we don't need to be directed by others in order to know our own nature. This is *self-realization*. We have actually discovered for ourselves that our nature is this universal Being.

Hence we have this autonomous, continuous unfoldment of our finite nature, without losing connection to that infinite field of Being which is arising as us. And so we are whole, in that sense.

Moreover the other is whole too — they are unfinished in their finite nature, as each of us are, but *whole* because they too are the unique individual expression of infinite Being, just as we are. There is no longer the demand that they "should be different." They are already complete, in this sense.

So when we meet this mysterious other who is whole too, there is awe! The awe arises unhindered because we don't need them to be different in order to be okay ourselves, and therefore we can discover the mystery of existence in the expression of *each* individuality.

PART II

Living Awakened Relationship

10

New Principles of Relationship

". . . rather than two people coming together
out of the need to be well and whole,
we are actually coming together
out of curiosity — and delight!"

IN OUR INCREASING wholeness, personal relationships can begin to operate on different principles. We are not meeting and getting into relationship with this mysterious other out of the need to be well and whole. There is no way that the other could ever fulfill that fundamental need, even though we had hoped so in the individuating stage of life. But now we know they can't. And we wouldn't want them to, because that would interfere with us. It would limit our wholeness.

In this new field, we begin to get to know this other person who is different from someone we might previously have chosen — different because in the past we may have chosen a person who we hoped was going to fulfill our needs. But now we are just meeting a mysterious other who, for mysterious reasons, has come across our path. (And I'm talking now in particular about special friendships, or intimate relationships.) The reasons are 'mysterious' because the truth is we didn't know them when we were born, and here they have arrived in our life. Something happens — circumstances, familiarities, similarities, compatibilities perhaps — and we meet this other. And, in coming into relationship, rather than two people coming together out of the need to be well and whole, we are actually coming together out of curiosity — and delight!

It's as if we were to exclaim, "Wow! The mystery is arising as *this* person!", just as we might walk through a flower garden, and, looking at a red rose, say to ourselves, "Wow! This flower is amazing!" And then we see the yellow daisy, and the truth is we don't want it to be the red rose, it's actually the yellow daisy, and yet, "Wow! It's beautiful too!" And so we acknowledge it. But then there's the green grass. It isn't even a flower. And yet it strikes us too with its own beauty.

So we begin to have that innocence which asks, "What's this one like?" And I might notice that, actually, right now, I'd rather be walking among the daisies, and that's my mood or perhaps more my nature. It's not because the grass isn't sufficient, or the roses aren't, it's because this is my inclination right now: I'm attracted to the daisies.

It's like that with people too: we get a certain freedom to be innocent in meeting and discovering them. And when we want to deepen in relationship with another, now the principles are different. We are no longer trying to create a relationship out of our mind, our weaknesses, or an image of our desires; we are meeting the other in a way that is open to discovery, evolution, and trust in our feeling nature.

11

11

Beyond Our Imaginings

"When we are whole, we have a chance to really see this strange other who has appeared in our life, . . . someone who is simply magical."

TYPICALLY, IN THE INDIVIDUATING self stage of life, a relationship requires both people cooperating to meet a pre-imagined form, which asks both of us to fit within it. And of course, in that paradigm, we want the relationship to fit the mould, we want it to work out, we want to evolve and progress, expanding our boundaries and cooperating more fully with the other — but, in fact, in some ways, we are trying to meet a form that is coming out of our own mind. It's like creating the daisy or the rose from a design we've made. It would have a frozen quality, because it's all we know, and we want to form it in a certain way. So then, if we could do that, we might find that every daisy looks identical. And every flower looks alike.

In this earlier paradigm of relationship, we were likely trying to form something that would resolve our individual developmental needs. Whereas when we are whole, we know we are not going to have those needs solved by relationship, at least in terms of compensation for our weaknesses and our losses. However, we may fulfill our needs in terms of our complement. That's different from unconsciously bringing our weaknesses to be solved through the agency of the other.

When we are whole, we have a chance to really see this strange other who has appeared in our life. Their strangeness comes from the fact that we don't know exactly what it's like to be them. And it seems we won't ever know. In addition, they may not appear like what we would have wanted or imagined at an earlier stage of our life. But, even so, we find someone who is simply magical. All the more so because we haven't created them in our own mind, and we are allowing them to be who they are while we cooperate in relationship. And even if we choose to compromise and take on certain roles, we are not doing it to exclude our individuality anymore. We know our own nature, so that is no longer doable. So then, if we want to work with another, to create a living situation with that different other, the cooperative aspect is more like gifts to each other, or even gifts to ourselves. It's a way into full enjoyment of being with each other, without depriving us of being well and whole.

12

Deepening in Wholeness
Through Relationship

"Intimate relationship is one of the places . . .
to discover more and more
that dimension of our wholeness
— or allness."

LET ME EMPHASIZE that we are finite in our individuality, so I'm not saying that we are autonomous in our *finite* nature. In our finite nature, we have certain things that we prefer: we like a tidy house, or we like a certain style of eating and so on. So we acknowledge our individual character. And that's a very tricky place in relationship, because our individuality does have needs and interests. Not to mention the fact that moving into our autonomous awakened nature doesn't mean we are finished, and doesn't mean we are wound-free. It just means that we are principally available to wholeness and self-recognition. So intimate relationship is one of the places that puts the most demand on us to discover more and more that dimension of our wholeness — or allness.

What I've discovered in becoming more well, whole and integrated is that there are some fundamental codependencies that continue to be in my nature, and which I've never recognized. In deepening into the experience of love relationship, I uncovered a subtle belief that the other is responsible for how I feel. And, on account of that, I have an expectation they should be behaving in certain ways. I started to notice this, and it really surprised me. It's almost unconscious, this subtle current, which says, "Of course they should!" And then I started to realize that this points to a place where I'm not autonomous. There's a way I'm saying that my happiness or my wholeness is dependent on the other.

So, in relationship, I'm realizing parts of me that are not whole, not integrated, not conscious. As I notice them, I can take time with them, honoring them, recognizing that, yes, I need the other person to do this and that, and that in some ways I feel less whole in that particular place. This then becomes my practice ground, if you like. And, in bringing these pieces to my attention, that relationship is a gift to me. Then, when I'm feeling whole again, or at least aware of that ground of wholeness, I still might not like the other person's behavior. Perhaps it feels like it's not harmonious or not in our agreement. But no longer is my response coming from that place of fundamental codependence.

13

Transformation Through Awareness

". . . we discover that this new approach
brings resolutions and integrations
we didn't previously know how to accomplish."

MOST OF THE DEVELOPMENT in awakened relationship seems to happen through awareness — through both personal and mutual awareness.

In contemporary relationship approaches, the development of the relationship requires a lot of talking, a lot of mutual understanding and a lot of agreements. Some of the teachings in the field of relationship advise us to never let something go unless it's finished, to always solve it, always try and meet it. They advise us to never leave angry, and so on and so forth. The inference is that both people are willing, able and ready to solve something at any point. But this is just not the case.

In our individual process in whole-being realization work, rather than try to fix, overcome or perfect ourselves, we learn to *greenlight* our current personal nature. Hence we give ourselves the go-ahead to be limited and hurt just the way we are for a while, so that we can deepen with awareness beyond the surface hurts into the deeper hurts, and ultimately into being our paradoxical nature of both finite and infinite. In this work, we find that our ability to use this approach effectively benefits greatly from receiving skilled coaching support. We would like to be fixing and healing these limits and hurts, however, after years of not accomplishing that fully, we come to discover that this new approach brings resolutions and integrations we didn't previously know how to accomplish.

In relationships too, when there are discomforts, we are in the habit of wanting to fix or heal them. Discomforts naturally arise because we are each individuals with our own hurts, tastes, needs and desires, and these just can't be ignored. At the same time, we each want to be in harmony with the other, living with them in love and enjoying their company, but it turns out many of the conflicts and discomforts that arise we simply *don't know how to solve*.

Here are two innocent parties, then, who are just being themselves. This includes their residual weaknesses, hurts, limits, and habits. And the whole-being realization process is unfolding, but not fundamentally through fixing, correcting, and so on. Instead, the partners honor themselves and each other as they are. They give themselves an opportunity through *greenlighting* to move more deeply, with awareness, into a condition where they find those things that are uncomfortable, that are barriers, dropping away, being resolved, or becoming integrated in their larger whole-being nature.

And so, with this approach, we start to find a growing sense of trust in awareness as a catalyst for our mutual transformation.

14

Evolutionary Awareness

". . . we find, over and over again,
that these things miraculously
release, transform, and integrate. . . ."

A RELATIONSHIP IS LIKE another being that's evolving.

And *awareness* is actually what's been evolving us and bringing our whole-being nature to light.

As we come into whole-being realization and awakened life, it's more inherent in our nature to trust the next discomfort that arises, to say to our self, "Oh yeah, here's another part of me that's not evolved, that's still wounded." We can then treat it with 'greenlighting' (*giving it the go-ahead to be that way for now*) or, more specifically, with 'evolutionary awareness' (*seeing it, feeling it, being it,* and *evolving through it*). These fundamental stages of evolutionary awareness were originally realized and expressed by spiritual teacher and Human Sun Institute co-founder Linda Groves-Bonder, in a process she calls Six-Step Recognition Yoga™.

Evolutionary awareness is a sequence of deepening levels of awareness that reflect the natural evolution of Being in creation. When a discomfort or pressure arises in our life, we can allow our awareness to deepen into it to bring about an evolutionary resolution. The natural sequence of deepening awareness proceeds through:

- ◦ 'seeing it' — awareness of what it is

- ◦ 'feeling it' — awareness of how it feels

- ◦ 'being it' — awareness of living as it

- ◦ 'evolving through it' — spontaneous emergence of greater wholeness and balance with it.

By consciously allowing awareness of our discomfort to deepen through these stages over time, we are cooperating with its natural evolutionary unfoldment, which is enlivened and supported through our awakened awareness.

This evolutionary awareness sequence progresses through the centers of awareness in our head, our heart and our belly, giving access to deeper layers of our being. It permits us to simply acknowledge what is occurring and give it the space to unfold through us. Thus, we cooperate with the discomfort without initially changing it. During this process it can be very helpful to have someone qualified to coach us through these subtle steps and transitions.

So we notice our discomfort (this is the 'seeing it' stage), and we might say, "Oh, this is awkward! I want to fix it...."

"But no, I'm going to give it time...."

"Okay, now I'm deepening into the feeling of it" (this is the 'feeling it' stage).

"Urrghh! It's horrible!"

"Okay, well now I know what it feels like, I should change it because I really don't like it...."

However, we have already come to recognize that we need to include *seeing* it, *feeling* it, and also *being* it, by living with and as that discomfort in its current form (this is the 'being it' stage). It may not make sense in personal development fields normally, but in this whole-being development, we are actually trusting Being to come alive by bringing awareness into the depths of the experience.

In awakened life, evolutionary awareness becomes second nature. It becomes the way life works. So we surrender to being it — by being the whole of the uncomfortable experience *with awareness*. And *heart*. And *trust*. And *holding*. Moreover we find that *talking* about it with trusted others as it is going on deepens our awareness into it. Speaking about it isn't to solve it — it is to bring more self-honoring and self-recognition to the whole dimension of what it's like to have that experience.

And then we find, over and over again, that these things miraculously *release, transform,* and *integrate within us* (this is the 'evolving through it' stage). There is less and less to do, because we are allowing this potent nature of Being that we have realized to unfold us. And it has always been doing this. Only, in this whole-being realization and awakened life, we are moving into a place of knowing, where we allow life to do its evolution — *to grow its plant as us*, in a sense.

15

From Solving to Evolving

*"In the being of the relationship . . .
we bring simple awareness, through greenlighting
and evolutionary awareness."*

IN THE BEING OF the relationship, there are many things that we don't know how to fix, with respect to the *discomforts* that we experience. In fact, neither party knows how to fix them, because both people are actually being themselves just as they are right now — with their hurts, limits, habits, and so on. So what do we do? Well, we bring simple *awareness* through 'greenlighting' and 'evolutionary awareness' in the way I previously described. And eventually these approaches become so automatic, we no longer need to consciously choose them, we are just *aware*, *allowing* and *transforming*.

Thus, we trust life to evolve our awakening or awakened relationship. We trust life *to grow its plant as the being of our relationship*.

We can't necessarily recommend this way of operating to people who haven't begun to find trust in their own unfoldment, in the way those awakening through mutuality-based whole-being realization work normally do. It wouldn't make sense, and it wouldn't be right to speak exactly in this way to people in that situation. But, in whole-being awakened realization and awakened relationships, we inherently know that we are *not* ready or able to solve many things — and so, instead, we allow them to evolve.

16

Discriminating What's My Stuff

". . . I can identify that this discomfort
really feels like it belongs to me,
and I know I need to allow it to evolve."

IN AWKWARD PLACES in relationship, and in my own experience with intimate love relationship in particular, one of the things I've discovered is that I can often recognize when some of my discomfort is actually *my own stuff*. These are my own hurt places that are feeling awkward, uncomfortable or unmet in certain ways. They don't belong to the other — they're mine. Because I am more well and whole now, I can identify that this discomfort really feels like it belongs to me, and I know I need to allow it to evolve. In this instance, 'greenlighting' and 'evolutionary awareness' are my work.

It might be helpful to speak to my partner, but it may trigger them, and it may sound like I'm blaming. And I may end up using a certain tone because I'm still experiencing the wound. So I might or might not choose to talk about it with the other — because it's really not theirs to solve. It's my process, and I need to give it space. And the remarkable thing is that it's the relationship that prods me into recognizing this unconscious piece — which is mine. And now I have the opportunity to take time with it. I have grown to trust this process, and it's become my automatic nature to just allow it to evolve.

Sometimes the process goes something like this, and the place of discomfort dissolves, and sometimes I keep finding the discomfort recurring for months, but even so I still know it's mine, and it has to have its time to mature and integrate.

Alternatively, sometimes I find that the issue really does seem to belong to the other. Maybe they are behaving in a way that's hurting me, or is uncomfortable for me, and this time it really feels like it's their stuff. I'm recognizing that they are acting out of their own wounding or confusion, and no amount of words is going to change that — because it's *simply true for them in this moment.* And so, am I going to try and work it out with them if, in fact, it's simply their nature at this point? If the relationship is strong and meaningful enough, then this is one thing that I want to allow to grow. And I'm already loving this person as a mysterious other, so I hold this piece as part of the mystery — and it just isn't mine to fix in any case.

17

Honoring the Discomforts in Relationship

"Held by this love,
the hurt and confusion can . . .
be given time to mature and evolve."

SOMETIMES THE ISSUES that arise seem to be clearly inter-mingled issues of the relationship. In this case we can apply the approach of 'evolutionary awareness' within the couplehood.

It turns out that it is valuable for the other to know the dis-comfort that is arising in me from their behavior or from the nature of our personal differences, and vice versa. And it's help-ful for us to express it into *the shared space of relationship* in such a way that it's offered *without expectation of immediate solution*. When both parties honor this process of unfoldment in which some things are not yet ripe to be solved — when both parties are operating in this paradigm — then they become familiar with sharing discomforts and allowing them to perco-late. And when we are interconnected with someone through the magic of circumstances (attraction, chemistry, commonali-ties and so on), when these have brought us into a shared expe-rience of a bond of love, that bond then becomes what holds us together while we feel confused or hurt by the particular painful circumstances. Held by this love, the hurt and confusion can therefore be given time to mature and evolve.

The catch is that we cannot control the process — any more than we can control our own individual awakening process. Once we might have said, "Now I see it, and I *have* to fix it, because I don't want to live like that anymore!" We wanted to manage it. That's what we'd been doing in the individuating self paradigm, and in doing so we progressed, we made space for some evolution and some healing. But in this whole-being paradigm we can't just say, "Okay, I *see* this wounded place in myself, now I've got to fix it." We actually have to *evolve* it. And that's typically by bringing awareness — which includes *feeling* and *living* right into it.

So, in relationship we are faced over and over with this very dilemma of something important being uncomfortable, and recognizing that it's not a mistake, it's not that the other is mean or unfair — it's actually a significant component of their nature. And my response to them is an integral component of my nature. In both cases, we don't know how to fix it right now. It is a big gift to ourselves and to the other when we can honor that and give it time to mature through our *mutual evolutionary awareness*.

If we are with someone who doesn't feel this dynamic quality of evolution in the relationship, and nor do they experience the truth of wanting to be together, then that would be a different dynamic. But here we are talking about a relationship where two people, who are awakened or awakening, are both knowing their connection and trusting life to unfold. This means there is no guarantee it's going to be comfortable, nor that it's going to have a certain timeline, and nor is there a guarantee that the relationship will ultimately be compatible. Even so, we come over time to deeply trust life always unfolding us for our best next step of evolution. And we become braver in our trust of that which we can't control.

18

Giving to the Other

"...I can give ...
without giving away myself."

AS WE'VE SEEN, there are places of discomfort which show up in a relationship that we don't know how to fix. At the same time, there are many things I *can* do to cooperate with the other at the level of the finite. Some of them may not be my nature, and I might not be inclined to do them, but I'm well enough to offer them as a gift. After all, I'm whole in myself, and it doesn't take away from me to do it. And I want to give gifts to my love! Moreover, I can give them without giving away *myself*.

There are some things, of course, which are just difficult, and people in relationship work hard at the mechanics of them. These mechanics may have to do with simple things like cooperating around what time is quiet time in your house, or around what kind of food or drinks you feel compatible with having or making for each other. These are practical things. In earlier times, differences around these things might have signified the failure of the other to fulfill us, but when you're not confused about your wholeness, you're not confused about these things meaning there is a lack of something. You are simply honoring yourself and your own needs while meeting those of the other.

19

Speaking Up for Myself

". . . it's actually my job
— indeed, my honorable duty! —
to acknowledge my wants and needs
as an individual."

THERE'S AN IMPORTANT aspect of this 'honoring of one's needs' that I haven't spoken about yet, which has come to light in my own process. It's been a surprise to me to discover in a new way that I have my own needs and wants as an individual. I've spent my life in the fields of education, training, social and community development; my character inclines naturally towards wanting to help others, and I'm less focused on looking after myself or my own needs. So, being in an awakening relationship, it's my nature to want to please the other and to want to give to my love what she wants. I love her, so I want to do that. And yet I've found myself surprised by the fact that I'm not satisfied with *just* serving the other — I also have this need, or this want. And so, in the discomfort of that situation, who is going to speak up for me? And, more than that, *how is my partner ever going to get a whole person if I am willing to give myself away and never be there in my wholeness?*

Therefore, it's actually my job — indeed, my honorable duty! — to acknowledge my wants and needs as an individual. And it's tricky ground, because my needs are sometimes confusedly involved in my wounds. This is a tough place. In becoming more well and integrated, I've found that, if I can hold these things long enough to allow them to mature, then, when I do speak out my needs, the expression of them is not completely overwhelmed by my wounds, my hurts, my complaints and accusations. But, if it happens that I do speak up sooner, this becomes part of the process of their evolution, and I don't mind doing that if I have to. It's honorable — in the sense that, "This is me." Even so, it's perhaps preferable when I can allow it to evolve and allow some of the confusion in me to evolve through awareness, and then speak it out when it's more mature.

It's been surprising to me to note this development towards acknowledging my nature and my needs as an individual. And when I do speak up for my needs, its not that they are spiritually high and perfect. Its more basic than that. I'm simply declaring, "This is a fundamental thing about me and I need to say it." Nonetheless, in saying it I have no way to force the other to get it. In fact, the chances are that they are *not* likely to get it — at least not then! And that's because they really are a different person. So, I'm saying it, but I'm actually saying it without expecting short term resolution. I'm just honouring myself: "This is bothering me... it just is." And it feels like a need, at this time. And there may be an inference that the other is supposed to fulfill it, but we already know that the other can't necessarily do that — that is, if we are with someone we can trust as being who *they* are.

20

Meeting the Unknowable in the Other

". . . more and more we find ourselves in
deeper love and admiration,
that has nothing to do with
whatever was the initial issue."

THERE IS A SURPRISING, confusing, but delicious dimension of evolving relationship: that an awakening or awakened relationship is not 'oneness' in the way that we may have often thought. It's not 'merging' in the ways that we have traditionally been told. It's actually having two autonomous beings who become interconnected and even interdependent — but in their wholeness. So this path, then, is richly full with *meeting the abyss of relationship, the unknowable or seemingly unacceptable in the other*, precisely because, as awakened divinely human individuals, we do still have our own finite identity with our own wants and needs, and so does the other.

So from what I can see, there is a *healthy need* to meet our sense of the unknowable or unacceptable in the other, and be fully present with it. There we find that the relationship we have is actually a dynamic that can go beyond where our hurts, our discomforts, or our personality traits are. It seems that the unconscious, subtle wounds and needs of our lifelong unfoldment get to be experienced most clearly when we want to be with someone because of our love, admiration, and interconnectedness, and it turns out that *they don't meet us* in the finite ways we had consciously or unconsciously hoped for. This leaves us faced again with realizing our own autonomous awakened nature. That's a priceless encounter! It's valuable because, at the subtlest levels of those needs, we may want to merge, we may want the other to save us.

Somehow, in relationship, and intimate relationship in particular, we are touching into subtler and subtler unconscious places, and, when we are fundamentally whole, we can meet our sense of the unacceptable or the unknowable in the other and not run away and not try to fix them. We are well enough to say,

"Let's see how this turns out." And I find in each of those times that have arisen for me that somehow I digest it — and so does the other. And more and more we find ourselves in deeper love and admiration that has nothing to do with whatever was the initial issue.

There are no clear-cut answers then. We are actually finding our own being's way in. We're dealing with the mysterious other who is both well and not well, and ourself who is both well and not well. As our wholeness and integration grows, when discomfort arises we have the immediate recognition that *this is the gift of the next meeting with our own discomfort*. And awakening and awakened relationship is the final frontier, you could say, of meeting the unknown — meeting *our* unknown — and, in that process, coming forward to honour ourselves and honour the other.

We can then gift each other with compromises or co-operation, gifts that no longer take away from our nature but are actually the joy of love.

21

From Oneness to Allness

". . . we have actually awakened
to the interconnectedness of our nature
— and all of nature."

DO WE NEED the other if we are autonomously awakened in our whole being nature? Well, it turns out that *I* do. I need the other in order to experience *more* wholeness — more wholeness *living as my individual self* that is. It doesn't seem to make any sense if I am already whole in myself, but it does make sense if we are engaged in the dynamic of living a manifest life. Then this wholeness is not simply a static or completed thing, but precisely *the manifestation of the interconnectivity that we have realized and are living*. It's not just *oneness* — it's *allness*.

We have realized the infinite field that arises as All, and we've realized the diversity of its manifestation, which is also still the *same material* — not better or worse. So we are living in relationship — whether we are in intimate relationship or not — and we have awakened to the *condition* of mutuality. This 'mutuality' doesn't mean that we behave or have to behave in a certain way, but means that we have actually awakened to the interconnectedness of our nature — and *all* of nature.

22

The Realization of Mutuality

"This is where
the interconnectedness
is undeniable."

IN THE CONTEXT of our interconnectedness with all nature, it's handy to know the practice of mutuality, which has been so fundamental to unfolding us as our conscious whole-being self. However, in many ways we are moving away from the 'doing' of mutuality and into the realization of it. This is where the interconnectedness is undeniable.

Interconnectedness exists when I don't like somebody as well as when I like them. I'm not disconnected because I don't like somebody — actually I'm *very* connected when I don't like somebody! So there is no such thing as 'not connected.'

Awakening to that knowing, I find that when I hurt somebody — because I say something, or I do something, or because they take something in a certain way — it actually matters to me personally. It's not just because of how they feel about me, but because I'm interconnected with them. And the more well I am in myself, then the interconnectedness just matters. So my behavior is not about acting appropriately according to what a 'code of mutuality' prescribes. The reality is that *I am in mutuality with everybody*.

I'm in mutuality in a way that doesn't require me to take on another's pain that is theirs, but even so, I really care about their pain. So, if they are affected by me in a way that I didn't intend, and even if I think it's their misunderstanding, that still matters to me. I'd like to be of help in ways that I can.

I can heartfully apologize for the discomfort they experienced and offer ways I can help to relieve the impact. I apologize because it matters to me that my being alive and my behaving in a certain way hurt the other. This has been referred to as 'coconut yoga' — symbolically my head bows down and hits the ground like a falling coconut, and my heart bursts open like the earth to deeply meet and hold the other in their discomfort.

This doesn't emerge from a need to appease them or from living the rules of mutuality — it comes out of our feeling nature. This feeling nature *is* the field of love.

23

Limits and Love

"We are deepening into the place
where our individuality . . .
is imbibed by love."

IN THE EARLIER life paradigm, we might have said, "I don't think I love that person... I really don't like what they're doing." The inference is that you have to like people to love them. And it makes sense. But it just isn't the reality we have awakened to. Instead, we have awakened to this interconnected field, which initially might just feel like interconnectivity or non-separateness. But I've found that, for me, more and more, this field is permeated with the flavor of *love*. It *is* love. And we don't have to call it that if we don't feel that way about it — we can just call it 'interconnectivity.' But I use the word 'love.' And I've tried to avoid that word for quite a long time now, because it has connotations of doing certain things and feeling certain ways, but nonetheless it seems to me that it best expresses the *undeniable intimacy of all life, of all creation*.

We can only fully know that interconnectivity when we have honored our individuality and encountered our limits. The reality is I've been deeply humbled by encountering my limits. And at the same time the process has been strangely *connecting*. The more that I have consciously met my personal limits, my failings, and my discomforts, the more that I've felt brotherhood and sisterhood with everyone in existence.

Awakened mutuality then becomes the discovery of an awakened nature which is interconnected *and* self-realized. Both. Hence we find ourselves in relationship, in awakened mutuality, having a 'both/and': both autonomous individuality and the truth of the interconnectivity. If we find love keeping us together, and keeping us together because we are more and more open to the mystery of the other, then this is a deepening into the essence of manifest love. We are deepening into the place where our individuality — that will always feel limited and somewhat disconnected — is imbibed by love.

It is in this way that my wholeness is enhanced by being in relationship — being in relationship with my intimate love partner, for example, and also being connected with my children, my relatives, my friends, and so on. They all are different dimensions of interconnectivity.

Some people in their whole-being awakened nature are naturally inclined to live more in that field of interconnectivity, some more in the field of embodiment, and some more in the field of consciousness or transcendence, but there isn't a right way to be. The whole range is our nature. It happens that my individuality is enhanced and complemented by the difference of a mysterious other who has emerged in my life and mutually found this love attraction. In the process, we've discovered that the relationship itself is an evolutionary prodding into greater integration in awakened life. It's an entry into the conscious and discriminatively-awake nature of noticing and knowing both the difference of the other, and simultaneously the sameness (or commonness) of that which is arising as All.

24

Expressing Awakened Mutuality

". . . the love-trust connection is the activating ground for mutually supporting and opening to each other."

REWARDING RELATIONSHIPS in awakened life benefit from integration of our 'realized interconnectedness and love' within our *personal* nature. This provides a basis for us to inter-act with others in a way that includes appreciative recognition of the *finite* qualities and needs of our self, others and groups.

Whenever I meet others from this ground of interconnected-ness, I find it's essential to acknowledge and respect *my own individual nature* in order for my wholeness to be experienced in and through relationships. Likewise, in interactions with oth-ers, particularly when I am in a position of power or authority, it's essential to honor *the other's individual nature,* so they feel the sense of connectedness they need in order to open and be responsive.

Generally, when we meet and support friends and family, or when we serve others in their awakening unfoldment, we want to bring a nurturing approach that includes hearing, support-ing, respecting, accepting, and loving them. Yet at certain times, there may also be value in offering a more 'proactive' style of counsel or guidance.

Whenever we offer proactive feedback or direction to another, it is crucial to authentically, respectfully and feelingly connect with them *first*, before we offer our perspectives for them to consider. By bringing our awareness to our own (pos-sible) judgements, insecurities, and fears, and to any sense of 'authority-certainty', 'parental-knowing-best', or personal pref-erence we hold, we can consciously allow any of these to be out-weighed by the deeper sense of *love-connectedness* that we wish to bring to the interaction. Then, by tapping into our *admiration* for them in their *beautiful, innocent humanity and personal life process*, we can personally relate to them with this inner feeling quality. This will bring a deeper seeing, trusting, loving flavor that can create a shared space of meaningful connection. From this shared space, we can then find out more about the personal experience and needs of the other while leaving ourselves open to learning from them and having our perspectives change.

When offering feedback or direction, if we're blinded by our good intentions or by our responsibilities, it's possible to fall into 'old paradigm' authority or parenting styles that do not meet the other in mutual respect, and that express criticism, directiveness, or knowing-best. Instead, we can sensitively offer proactive support to the other through *inspiring* their creativity, *challenging* their self-exploration, and *coaching* their choice-making. These approaches can help illuminate alternative behaviors, initiatives and realizations that may serve them in their awakening lives. In these ways we *invite, encourage* and *empower* them to move forward with what resonates for them in their continuing evolutionary unfoldment. From our side, we bring our attunement to their experience and what we feel may be useful and receivable by them, and then we must trust in Being in its mysterious unfoldment through, as, and for them.

In the context of *awakened love relationship*, the *love-trust connection* is the activating ground for mutually supporting and opening to each other. Any input, feedback, or guidance to each other coming from this connecting ground will be flavored by the openness and love-trust that we share. When we feel more *separate* and act more *toward* the other, we may find ourselves in a position that feels more outside of the shared relationship space, more outside of our relationship love-trust field. When we re-open ourselves to that love-trust connection and find ways to see, hear, admire and trust the other, we bring a renewed sense of communicating *with* the other. This orientation respects and trusts each other's autonomous nature. Then what we offer to the other has space to be considered, to percolate within them, and to empower their own understandings and choices in their evolutionary course of life.

This expression of awakened mutuality arises from our integrated awakened nature, increases our experience of love-trust with life itself, and opens us to discover ourselves acting and growing in the nature of love.

PART III

Evolving in Fulfillment

25

Whole-Being Evolution™

*". . . a dynamic process of ever-unfolding
knowing, being and loving realization . . ."*

WHOLE-BEING EVOLUTION™ is a natural, lifelong process. It is occurring in our own life and throughout all life as an evolutionary impulse of Being.

Whole-being evolution leads progressively through emergence, immersion, personal development, and phases where we are awakening to the full range of our infinite and finite nature, and it continues endlessly in divinely human unfoldment, integration and expression.

The fundamental nature of the self has an inherent potential for evolutionary transitions. These unfolding transitions manifest and refine within us as a sequence of overlapping integrations, leading to increasing whole-being fulfillment.

Whole-being evolution is a dynamic process of ever-unfolding knowing, embodying, and loving realization, as we deepen as Consciousness, Being and Love.

As love is deeply realized and integrated throughout the impersonal, personal, and interpersonal realms of our realized self, we come to know, be and live as *whole-being love*.

Whole-being love™ in one person meeting whole-being love in another—this is the essence of fulfillment in awakened relationship.

26

Whole-Being Realization
Is a Quantum Shift

". . . awakening to the perfection
of our life
and all of life
— as it is."

ATTENTION TO OUR PERSONAL development is valuable and can go on continuously for the rest of our life. However, it is possible to awaken to our full nature at any point when we feel clearly ready to engage in whole-being realization work that supports deepening into our nature as it is. It is possible to open to our underlying potential for unfoldment into whole-being awakened life — not by working to develop our human perfection, but by awakening to the perfection of our life and all of life — as it is.

In whole-being, non-dual realization, we do not get to choose which parts of our self and the world we awaken to — we awaken to all of life as it is. Therefore, the doorway into our realization must be through our self, including the parts we have felt are wrong, not complete, not desirable — not to make them perfect but to live consciously into and through them. Each person is unique and therefore each person's awakening will be unique in the context of realizing their own individual nature simultaneously with their realization of the infinite wholeness of all that is. Our own individuality MATTERS as a divinely human aspect of manifest creation, as do our individual relationships with every other individual aspect of wholeness.

Whole-being realization to me is a true paradigm shift, a quantum leap. Life is moving us in that direction within the pace of our own nature and life circumstances. And we benefit from personal support and from actively leaning into mutual engagement with others, to accelerate our movement toward realizing and living awakened wholeness and non-separateness with all of life.

Beneficial personal support for whole-being realization includes:

- ○ Whole-being activation through our relationship with those who are living in integrated wholeness

- ○ Whole-being knowledge that can help us be with our self in new ways that hold paradox, embrace our imperfections, and support our stages of awakening

- ○ Whole-being coaching related to actual circumstances arising in our life, offered within an atmosphere of shared, respectful mutuality and trust

- ○ Whole-being workshops and retreats that include activation, knowledge, coaching, and mutuality

- ○ Whole-being mutuality in groups that are practicing mutual gazing, personal sharing, and interpersonal mutuality — as approaches that support whole-being realization and living and expressing in awakened life

The interconnected nature of all existence becomes deeply realized through whole-being realization that is inclusive of consciousness, embodiment and mutuality. We directly perceive our personal nature and all of existence as non-separately interconnected within a universal conscious field.

This conscious embodied non-dual realization offers a vital foundation of wholeness for living and evolving in awakened life and relationships.

27

Intensification of Whole-Being Realization

". . . as we come to consciously live . . .
as the core paradox, . . .
we can discover . . . the alchemical fire
at the source of our life."

THE PARADOX OF INFINITE and finite at the basis of our individual nature has been referred to in various ways, such as core wound, core paradox, existential discomfort, core mystery. These terms speak to a mystifying inner experience of the simultaneous coexistence of our *infinite* nature, and our *finite* nature, at the very core of our being.

Noticing this inner experience from the perspective of our finite individuality, it can feel like a wound, tension, confusion, angst, fear... something deeply wrong. Our conscious or unconscious experience of this fundamental discomfort has been a governing factor for most us in living our lives. This paradoxical inner discomfort has actually been a key propellant of human life-force within the individuating self — attempting to *heal*, *fix*, *escape*, *overcome*, or *be saved from* this underlying condition.

Yet the core wound paradox doesn't get to be resolved while we are alive and finite. In fact, we wouldn't want it to be resolved, because then we would be nothing — in a sense. To accede to the desire to resolve the core wound, the core paradox would be *to put out the fire of our own being*.

In my experience, as we come to consciously live in and as the 'core paradox' in our whole-being realized condition, we can discover this 'inner core' as the *alchemical fire at the source of our life*, the *Creation Point* of our existence. This brings a fundamental realization of... Wellness... Wholeness... Freedom... Love... Trust in Being... the Isness of Life.

In our awakened life, we continue to *deepen and integrate* in the ground of our awakened nature *by consciously holding the feeling sense of our alchemical core* while meeting the finite discomforts, confusions and challenges that arise in our daily lives. We also continue to *mature* in our awakened nature by *recognizing and expressing* our 'creative impulses', 'inner knowings', and 'loving feelings' that naturally emerge in our ongoing activities and relationships.

Over time, as we become increasingly conscious and deeply integrated in and as our whole-being nature, we can experience a further *transformative shift* in which the foreground of our finite experience becomes outshone by the penetrating *intensification of wholeness* at the core of our being. This intensification of our whole-being realized nature *burns within us* as a trinity of Consciousness, Being and Love, *expanding our knowing-awe* of the mystery of existence, *deepening our lived-experience* of trust in being, and *magnifying our feeling-sense* of the nature of love.

28

Living in Wholeness, Trust, and Love

*"We realize love . . .
as a discovery of the truth
of our own nature. . . ."*

WE'VE CONSIDERED how the paradox of infinite and finite at the core of our being can feel like a 'wound'. The experience of the 'core wound' can evolve through our whole-being realization process to a feeling of 'core wellness' and a knowing of 'core trust.' As we further integrate in our awakened life, we can discover this 'inner core' as the *alchemical fire of our life*, the *Creation Point* of our existence.

As we become increasingly conscious *in* and *as* the *inner core of our being*, we can come to recognize it as our *center* of *wholeness, trust and love*. That is, while consciously living as our alchemical core, we are aware of our 'autonomous awakened nature', we feel our deep 'inner wellness', and we realize our 'non-separate interconnectivity'.

Being aware of our *autonomous awakened nature* means that we have *realized* our conscious nature that is not dependent on a teaching, or on a particular person — or on anything else. We have actually realized our *wholeness*, and we have realized it through our individuality. And we have done that because we have discovered that our individuality is not separate from that wholeness, or Allness.

Perception of our *inner wellness* and our sense of *trust in Being* emerge as we deeply *experience* our alchemical core in which Consciousness, Being, and Love synergistically arise as our *self* and all else, and we realize all is occurring and included within our own nature.

We realize our *awakened interconnectivity* through having *discovered* the non-separate nature of our self and all-that-is, while at the same time recognizing the finite difference of the other. We are recognizing their autonomous nature, as well as the non-separate interconnection between us — which to me *is love*.

We *realize love*, not as a behavior or as a teaching, but as a discovery of the truth of our own nature, in our own being, and in connection with all and everything.

Through this awakening unfoldment of our *self*, we discover our inherent *trust in Being* and find that *wholeness* and *love* are our nature. In discovering this full nature of our self, we honor the value of the *separation,* sense of *wound*, and *co-depen-dence* that we may experience on the way, because these are the elements of that which is evolving in us now — emerging in a new form and in a new fulfillment, as Wholeness, Trust, and Love.

Over time, our *intensifying* whole-being realized nature becomes an increasing beacon of wholeness and love for all and everyone through the interconnected field of collective con-scious mutuality.

In the *shared bond* of an *awakened relationship*, wholeness, trust, and love emerge in an increasing experience of *lived-wholeness*, and a growing realization of *mutual love-trust*. Awakened relationship becomes a catalytic field of healing, transformation, enrichment, and fulfillment that evolves and rewards each and all of us.

29

Awakened Relationship

*". . . we discover new ways of interpreting relationship,
and new principles of evolving relationship. . . ."*

AS WE AWAKEN to our inherent heart-awakened nature, we can discover ourselves *being* love. This is our essence. I'm not expressing this as a kind of instruction, so that others need to go looking for it. I think that we discover our love-nature in our whole-being awakened realization when we deeply realize Being in and as the conscious fabric of our lives.

When we are living in whole-being heart-awakened life, and when we are in relationships with others, then to me, we are being *in* love and living *in* love. And being in love and living in love reflects our awareness *in* love that is inclusive of the manifest and unmanifest realms of life.

In heart-awakened mutuality, we are living our awakened non-separate interconnectivity (*living love*), experiencing manifest and unmanifest embodied within us (*being love*), and realizing our awakened conscious nature (*knowing love*). This beautifully reflects the spectrum of our love nature — which is inclusive of our relationships, our embodiment, and our awareness.

This comes to be lived in awakened relationship, where we discover new ways of interpreting relationship, and new principles of evolving relationship — principles which are founded in our nature as love, in our trust in Being arising as us and as the other, and in our realization of all-inclusive consciousness.

Whole-being heart-awakened relationship evolves in fulfillment through the shared bond of whole-being love.

Afterword

". . . I am most gratefully surprised to find myself
. . . in the midst of a divinely human
intimate love relationship . . . ."

I CAN VERY PERSONALLY relate to the yearning for a deeply connected intimate love relationship that I know so many people feel. So I am most gratefully surprised to find myself in this stage of my life in the midst of a divinely human intimate love relationship with my beloved wife, Andrea Bruecks.

How did this happen?!? I would say it started with my experience of a deep relationship heartbreak, worse than anything I could have imagined, that occurred for me many years ago. This became the catalyst that ultimately led me, through healing processes and conscious embodied awakening work, to my whole-being realization and my subsequent years of integrating in increasing wholeness.

During these years of integration in the midst of my particular constraining life circumstances, I came to surrender to not having an intimate partner. As I came to hold the discomfort of this absence, in the same way that I increasingly found I could hold the core wound/core mystery paradox at the center of my being, I unexpectedly dissolved out of the sharp yearning for an intimate love relationship, and I even dissolved out of all of my life-long specifics of what I had envisioned and yearned for in a relationship. I came into a sense of not believing or needing to believe in such a relationship for me and accepting I would not likely have one for the rest of my life.

Through these years of awakening integration, my experience also evolved into a deep recognition of my heart awakened nature *as love* — with a reverberation of heart-love throughout my body and realized consciousness seated in my heart, with all-that-is contained within my love. Later, when I found myself more fundamentally well-grounded in my awakened life, I was very surprised and deeply moved when I had an unexpected heart-opening shift into feeling myself as being per-sonally *loved by Being*...! Ahhhh..., how unexpected, how soothing, and how beautiful, after such a long earlier stage of transcendent-oriented life in which I had carried a deep uncon-scious sense of unworthiness!

With this shift, I continued to be aware of the possible growth and fullness that an intimate relationship might offer. However I was living this experience of loving and being loved in my awakened life, without any edge of yearning for a love partner, or any sense of needed partner qualities, or even any belief in having a love relationship again.

However, along came a beautiful woman in her awakened life, who cautiously announced to me that she loved me deeply and wanted to create a beautiful life-long love relationship with me! I had known Andrea very well for a couple of years, but only as a loving friend. I was distinctly surprised and felt very deeply touched by her declaration. There were initial life com-plications and a period of delay, but soon I said yes to "investi-gating" this surprising, very moving offer of love that arrived so beautifully in my life.

As I opened my inner doors to her, our relationship quickly changed from "investigating" to "being in" love relationship. My freedom from earlier love relationship desires, goals, and expectations, left me more open than I'd ever been to see and love the unique, beautiful other. And knowing myself as whole without any requirement for a love relationship, left me much more capable of meeting the abyss of the unknown or the unac-ceptable that can show up in an evolving relationship, without flinching, without acting, abiding in being, and discovering whatever is; leaving me free each time to discover the next opening and reaffirmation of deeper knowing love.

Andrea's confident unshakeable love has soothed my wounds and grown my trust, and is a fundamental current that anchors and nourishes our relationship. From the ground of this experience, I've been thrilled to find principles of awakening and awakened relationship coming into my view and trumping the orderly mechanics of contemporary relationship teachings. My residual fears, wounds, and broken zones that needed awakened relationship to shine a light on them, have been continually met and integrated through 'evolutionary awareness' in myself, and in the shared space of our relationship.

While an intimate awakening and awakened love relationship will naturally be healing and transformative, this love relationship has come at a stage in my awakened life in which I experience it more predominantly as bringing life enrichment and fulfillment. While it can be very challenging at times, and confusion about self, other, and relationship can arise, I experience it more continually as a fun, rewarding, sharing, juicy, illuminating, fulfilling, love companionship.

At times when I am on my own, I find myself naturally residing more in the direction of transcendent emptiness in my conscious embodied realization. When I am with my love Andrea, I feel myself brought much more into a living embodied experience of my awakened nature. Not that I am changed in my fundamental character, but this complement of her residing more in the direction of embodiment in her awakened realization, enriches the wholeness of my lived experience in awakened life.

My deepest love and gratitude flow
to my beautiful love Andrea,
and to Being as it expresses
through, as, and to me.

About the Author

ROD TAYLOR has been teaching spiritual awakening knowledge and techniques for over 40 years. He is currently a teacher of Trillium Awakening educational offerings and coaching services and Pan Gu Shengong qigong. Rod has a Master's Degree in Adult Education and post-secondary certification in Conflict Resolution. He lives in British Columbia, Canada.

In 2005, Rod experienced a fundamental shift into non-dual conscious embodied awakening. He realized his infinite, non-separate wholeness, simultaneously integrated with his finite nature of individual self. He now loves working with others to support their processes of whole-being realization and their deepening integration in their awakened nature as Consciousness, Being and Love.

Rod came into love relationship with his beloved wife, Andrea Bruecks, MD, in 2010. Nourished by their love, this relationship became the catalyst for his recognition of new principles of awakening and awakened relationship. Rod offers workshops, and individual and couple sessions, to help participants recognize principles of awakened relationship and implement approaches to living awakened mutuality in their own lives.

You can contact Rod at:
awakened.relationship@gmail.com

Find out more about Rod and his services at:
www.awakeninginwholeness.com
trilliumawakening.org/profile/rodtaylor/

About the Editor

RALF HUMPHRIES LIVES in Melbourne, Australia, and is a senior clinician at a residential drug and alcohol rehabilitation facility, where he facilitates groups and works one-on-one with individuals. He also teaches in an undergraduate program that trains psychotherapists and art therapists, and is a therapist in private practice.

Ralf has been engaged with whole-being awakening work, through Waking Down in Mutuality and Trillium Awakening programs, since the middle of 2011. He has been working with Rod Taylor as his primary teacher since December, 2011.

In May 2013, Ralf was walking along a forest path near his home and, coming out of a stream of thought, he noticed that something was different. Things were somehow brighter and more luminous, more present in an inexplicable way. As he walked into a clearing and saw the tall redgum trees standing by the river's edge, it became apparent to him that something had shifted.

"I am All of this," he realized.

"How for a moment, for a split second, for the tiniest instant of awareness, could I not be All of this?"

A short time later, one of Saniel Bonder's words came to him. "Seamless". For a while, he searched for a 'seam' separating him from the world, or things from other things, or his consciousness from the consciousness of everything, but he couldn't find one anywhere.

As night fell, he tested his new awareness by looking at a far away star, and even though it was unimaginably far, still there was no line of separation anywhere. Though clearly separate entities, he and the star were undivided from each other.

And then there was no attraction to test anymore. It was just true. He *was* All of this—all the way from right here to infinity.

This whole-being realization has not left him, but continues to bring new depths of discovering love and fulfillment.

Ralf has a background that includes work as a musician, creative writing, doctoral research in the philosophy of paradox, program development for training integrative therapists, and a five-year period of intensive meditative practice as a Buddhist monk in the lineage of the Thai Forest Tradition.

You can contact Ralf at:
  ralfhum@gmail.com

Or find out more about Ralf and his services at:
  www.ralfhumphries.com.au

Disclaimer

Rod Taylor is a human development teacher. He is not a certified psychotherapist and this material should not be considered a substitute for psychotherapy or relationship counselling.

www.ingramcontent.com/pod-product-compliance
Lightning Source LLC
LaVergne TN
LVHW051347080426
835509LV00020BA/3329